Ruby Lane

Jenifer Stroud

Copyright © 2018 Jenifer Stroud

All rights reserved.

ISBN: 198616554X
ISBN-13: 978-1986165549

DEDICATION

This is for the Songwriters,
You were always my poets for as long as I can remember.
For my son, Galen Lonergan who makes my world brighter.
And last but in no way least, My Muse.
You set me on fire with one word…Lovely.
And that flame became a bonfire.

ACKNOWLEDGMENTS

About my poetry.
I don't write because I hate you or I'm angry.
Or that I need to keep you at arm's length.
Or that I'm too broken to be or know love.
words flow up in me like tidal pools with their own current.
Emotional riptides that sometimes take me by surprise in their urgent furious tempo wanting to be heard like gremlins crawling out of my own Pandora's box.
Know this, to have any strength those words had to come from a place where you were and always will be loved.
2/28/2016

You are Golden -
I've been living on the essence of dreams
for too long now
sifting their dust between my fingers
leaving them caked
with all the hopes I shared with you
they smell like desire and fiery ember still
golden trails fall to the floor
and my hands are too full to catch them
I take a deep breath
and blow them all away
letting the wind carry them to You.
11/26/2009

STARS ARE DRIPPING DOWN
FROM HEAVEN
AND POOLING IN YOUR EYES
I WATCH THEM THERE
TWINKLING THEIR SECRETS
BEWITCHING THE CORNERS
OF YOUR SMILE
AS I CHASE THEM
I AM FALLING
AND YOU GAVE ME WINGS
SO I COULD REACH THEM.
3/01/2016

YOUR IMAGE HELD
IN TWILIGHT MEMORY
NOSTALGIA FRAMED
IN THE FIRE LIGHTS GLOW
I'M TURNING TO EMBERS
IN THE RECOLLECTION
SET ABLAZE
BY KNOWING YOU.
2/18/14

IT'S NOT THAT I'VE FORGOTTEN
WHAT YOU MEAN TO ME,
BUT MY FITHY MIND IS RACING
TO THE POINT OF RELEASE,
I'M WOUND TIGHTER
THAN AN OLD BED SPRING
& THE TENSION IS BUILDING
OUT HERE IN THE HEAT,
I JUST NEED A DOSE OF SATISFACTION
TO AIL WHAT'S WRONG WITH ME,
& I CAN TELL BY HIS SMILE
HIS JEANS HOLD ALL THAT I NEED.
3/02/12

IN YOUR EYES
I SEE POSSIBILITY
AND FEEL LIKE
I'M HOLDING YOUR HAND
I KEEP WISHING
THAT TIME WOULD GO SLOWLY THEN
BECAUSE I DON'T GIVE A DAMN
IF ANYONE KNOWS WHERE I AM
SO WE STAND
ON THE EDGE OF THIS PRECIPICE
AND WE SMILE AT DANGER IT HOLDS
DANCING INSIDE THE HINT OF THIS
WHILE TEMPTATION HAS US IN TOW.
2/16/2017

MY HAND IS STAINED
THE COLOR OF YOUR LEAVING
I TOUCHED THE SPOT
WHERE YOU HAD BEEN
THIS HOLE IN MY HEART
IS SO DAMN OVERWHELMING
I DON'T KNOW IF I'LL EVER
FEEL WHOLE AGAIN.
2/11/2018

THERE ARE PEOPLE YOU WRITE TO,
THERE ARE PEOPLE YOU WRITE FOR,
& THOSE YOU WRITE WITH...
I HAD ALWAYS HOPED
THAT WE WOULD BE ALL THREE.
2/11/2018

I CAN'T SLEEP
WHEN I THINK
OF YOU NOT DREAMING
I CAN'T BREATHE
KNOWING I WASTED
ANOTHER DAY
I DON'T LOOK BACK
BECAUSE
OF THE CHANCE I WASTED
I WON'T LIE & SAY
I DON'T MISS YOU
EVERYDAY.
2/03/2018

BURIED HERE
UNDER MY FEAR
THESE JANGLING BONES
WHISPERING THIER SECRETS
INTO THE NIGHT
THEY ACHE & CONSPIRE
TO SET YOU ON FIRE
WHILE I FEEL THE END
OF MY ROPE
I WAS NEVER GOOD
AT APOLOGISES
THE WORDS ALWAYS
STRAYED AWAY
I WISH I FELT SAFE
WHEN STANDING IN PLACE
SO CLOSE
TO YOUR BECKONING HAND
2/12/20

I'M A SHARP TONGUE SERPENT
BUT I WON'T LICK YOUR BOOTS,
I'M COMING ON YOU SO FAST
YOU WON'T HAVE TIME TO MOVE,
I WILL SHAKE YOUR FOUNDATIONS SO HARD
YOU FORGET YOUR LOVERS NAMES,
AND LEAVING YOU IN THE MORNING
WONDERING WHY YOUR LIFE JUST ANIT THE SAME...
NO ONE ELSE HAS GOT A LOVE THIS FINE,
I'LL KEEP YOU CRYING FOR IT BABY,
A TASTE SWEETER THAN HONEY WINE...
COME AND TOUCH ME BOY,
YOU KNOW,
YOU WERE MENT TO BE MINE.
2/20/12

WHY IS IT THAT I WRITE
WHEN I CAN'T SLEEP?
THE DECADES HAVE PASSED
& THE WORLD KEEPS ON SPINNING
BUT THOUGHTS OF YOUR TOUCH
STILL BRING ME TO MY KNEES
AS I LIE HERE FETAL
AWAITING TO MY DREAMS.
1/29/2018

YOU BROKE MY HEART
& I BLED OUT
IN ANGER OVER TIME
LEAVING IT'S MIRYAD
OF SHADES IN MY WAKE
A COLORFUL PATH OF DESTRUCTION
WITH EVERY FOOTFALL
LEADING AWAY
FROM MY LOVES ONLY ACHE
1/29/2018

IN THE MIRRORS OF MY MIND
SHATTERED MOMENTS
ARE HELD IN TIME
A MYRIAD OF MEMORIES
ASLEEP AS THEY RESIDE
REMINDERS OF WHEN I FELT ALIVE
& I WOULD SWIM AGAIN
IN THAT SEA OF BLUE
FOR ANOTHER SMILE
JUST FROM YOU.
1/11/2018

MEMORIES LIE
BECOMING TWISTED OVER TIME
& WE'RE PUPPETS TO THIER CALL
I DON'T SEE THE REAL US THERE AT ALL

OVER & OVER IN MY HEAD
ALL THE PASSION
I THOUGHT DEAD
COMES BLEEDING OUT
AT THE SIGHT OF YOU

I ALWAYS DENIED
THIS PERFECT CRIME
LIKE ACCIDENTAL LOVERS
FROZEN IN TIME

BUT YOU WERE THE ONE THING
I COULDN'T RESIST
PULLED LIKE A MAGNET
TO YOUR CUNNING ABYSS

OVER & OVER IN MY HEAD
ALL THE PASSION
I THOUGHT DEAD
COMES BLEEDING OUT
AT THE SIGHT OF YOU

MEMORIES LIE
BECOMING TWISTED OVER TIME
TRYING TO REACH YOU
WAS MY FATAL FLAW
WHEN I DON'T SEE THE REAL US
THERE AT ALL
1/24/2018

THIS PENT UP SILENT SCREAM
THE HOLLOW ACHE
BEARING YOUR NAME
IT'S HEAVY WEIGHT
LOW IN MY BELLY
HUNG BY MY
MACRAME HEARTSTRINGS
THAT WHISPERS
EVERY TIME
I CLOSE MY EYES.
1/03/2018

I AM TIRED...
TAKE ME UP IN YOUR STRONG ARMS
& POSSESS MY SKIN
WITH YOUR FINGERTIPS,
LEAVE DESIRE'S FIERY TRAILS
IN THIER WAKE...
FEED THE EMBERS WITH YOUR KISSES
UNTIL I COMBUST
TURNING MY WATERY NATURE INTO STEAM
CLINGING
TO YOUR EVERY SATED CURVE.
4/03/12

YOU ARE GOLDEN
SHINING IN THE SUNLIGHT
EYES TURNED TOWARDS THE SEA
MIRRORING IT'S INTENSITY
YOU LOOK MY WAY
AND I AM BATHED
IN THEIR AQUATIC BLUE
I PAUSE MY BREATH
FEELING THE STRONG PULL
FEARING I WILL DROWN
IN THEIR UNDER TOW.
12/23/2013

MISMATCHED BLANKETS
AND KNEE SOCKS
FROZEN SHEETS
THAT MAKE MY KNEES KNOCK
SKIN IS SO COLD
YOUR TOUCH IS THE FLAME
AWAKENING TEMPTATION
AND FANNING THE FIRE.
2/25/2016

CLOSE MY EYES
INHALE AND BREATHE
IN THE MUSKY SCENT OF YOU
WARM WOOD
AND PROMISES
POLISHED STEEL VEINS
RUNNING ALONG YOUR FLESH
DARING MY FINGERS
TO EXPLORE YOUR APPEALING FRAME
YOUR BODY HUMS WITH EXCITEMENT.
8/28/2016

YOU'VE BEEN WALKING MY MIND
FOR AN ETERNITY
HAUNTING MY DARK HALLS
PRESENT IN MY SUNRISE
WHERE MY HOPE STILL GROWS
THERE IN THE GOLDEN SILENCE
I CAN STILL HEAR YOUR FOOTFALLS
THAT ECHO IS STILL SO BITTERSWEET.
4/27/2014

CRUMPLE THE PAGE
THROW IT AWAY
THAT'S A PART OF THE PAST
NO LONGER TODAY
FIGHTING A TIGER
I THOUGHT I COULD TAME
BUT I FELT IT'S TEETH
AND I'M NO LONGER THE SAME
I'M LOOKING FOR SHADOWS
WHILE STANDING IN SHADE
AFRAID OF MY TEARS
SO I CRY IN THE RAIN
I ACHE FOR LOVE
WHILE ONLY FIND PAIN
YET I REACH OUT AGAIN.
11/28/2016

YOUR LOOMING SHADOW
A BLANKETING CURSE
HELD IN IT'S EMBRACE
EVERYONE ELSE PALES
IN INTIMATE COMPARISON
WHILE YOU ARE
A LONG SWEET ACHE.
12/31/2016

DID YOU CATCH A GLIMMER
OF MY SOUL
FLOATING NEAR THE SURFACE
UP AGAINST
OUR DIFFERENCES
IN THE LUNAR LIGHT
DO YOU SEE
THE WAY I CAN'T HELP
BUT SHINE
WITH A MOMENT
OF YOUR TIME
SURROUNDING ME
SPINNING THROUGH MY MIND
1/10/2017

WE RAN BREAKNECK
FLYING DOWN THE ASPHALT
LOOKING FOR THAT WAY OUT
OF ALL THE TRAGEDY
WE HAVE KNOWN
AND NOW WE'RE YANKED BACK
TO REEVALUATE THAT ANGER
WHEN WE ARE FORCED TO REMEMBER
THAT DIAMONDS
LOOK A LOT LIKE BROKEN GLASS
1/10/2017

I CAN FEEL YOUR FINGERS DISENGAGE
YOU'RE BACKING AWAY
WORDS THAT ONCE FLOWED
COME HESITANTLY
YOU ARE MEASURING THE DISTANCE
BETWEEN PLEASURE & PAIN
AND FINDING THE EXIT
HARD TO RESIST
SO I TRY NOT TO CRY
WHILE I REMEMBER YOUR SWEETNESS
AND REMEMBER MY HEART'S NOT ON TRIAL.
1/20/2017

I NEED SOMETHING
THAT I CAN'T DENY
THE FEEL OF YOUR SKIN
YOUR TOUCH ON MY THIGHS
THE WHISPER OF PLEASURE
HIDDEN DEEP IN YOUR SMILE
THE WAY YOUR EYES READ ME
& LEAVE ME BEGUILED
1/20/2017

WORDS TUMBLING
FROM MY FINGER TIPS
SILENT ECHOES VOCALIZED
HOPES LAIN
WHERE MY DREAMS
ARE PINNED
BUTTERFLY SHADES
SHIMMERING
AWAITING YOUR GAZE
1/03/2018

YOU ARE MY ELOQUENCE
THE SHINING MUSE
MY CATALYST
AS THESE PRECIOUS WORDS
FLOAT TO THE SURFACE
TRYING TO EXPRESS
THE RADIANCE
I FIRST FOUND
IN THOSE BRILLIANT EYES.
1/01/2018

ANOTHER DAY
ANOTHER PATH
ANOTHER YEAR
WITHOUT YOUR LAUGH
ANOTHER TIME
ANOTHER PLACE
WITHOUT THE SMILE
UPON YOUR FACE
I GAMBLED ALL MY TOMORROWS
ON THAT SUNNY YESTERDAY
ALONE, I KEEP ON PAYING.
12/30/2017

I WAKE UP
& PULL THEM BACK IN
ALL THE MESSY PIECES
FLOATING WHILE I SLUMBER
ALL THE NEGATIVE SELF TALK
ALL THE JUDGEMENTS
ALL THE TINY FAILURES
THAT MAKE MY DAYS
I PULL THEM BACK IN
& WEAR THEM
I WEAR THEM AS AN ARMOR
TO HOLD BACK
ALL THE THINGS THAT I KNOW
I AM NOT.
12/28/2017

I KEEP HEARING YOUR FOOTSTEPS
IN FRONT OF ME
& TRY TO CATCH THEM
WONDERING IF YOU EVER GLANCE
OVER YOUR SHOULDER
LOOKING FOR ME
TO TURN THAT NEXT CORNER
OR FLASH YOU A SMILE
SO YOU'LL BE PATIENT WITH ME
THAT IT'S TAKING LONGER
THAN YOU EXPECTED
TO REACH THAT POINT
WHERE I SAY "WAIT! I'M RIGHT HERE"
AND I DO...BUT WHERE ARE YOU?
YOU'RE GONE
AND I CAN ONLY HEAR YOUR FOOTSTEPS.
12/22/2017

STANDING INSIDE MY HELL
ALL MY DEMONS DWELL
AS I SURROUND MYSELF
WITH A LIFE THAT ONLY MAKES ME WEEP
EVERY TIME THAT I REACH OUT
I'M PUSHED DEEPER INTO MY DOUBT
AS EVERYTHING I WANT JUST FALLS APART
I COULD BE IN THE EYE OF THE STORM
AND NEVER KNOW IT
BE IN LOVE BUT NEVER SHOW IT
BECAUSE HAPPINESS
ISN'T SOMETHING THAT I SEE
SO I WALK AROUND SO BLINDLY.
1/26/2017

PIXEL IMAGES
NEVER DO YOU JUSTICE
YOUR INNER LIGHT
GOES UNNOTICED.
AND STILL, I END UP ACHING
TO TOUCH YOUR FACE.
TO CARESS THOSE FEATURES
I KNOW SO WELL
LETTING MY THUMB
GENTLY STROKE YOUR BOTTOM LIP.
I BITE MY OWN REMEMBERING
SUCH INTIMACIES.
I FONDLY THINK OF OUR LAST KISS
IT'S THE ONLY NEW YEARS EVE MEMORY
I HAVE WORTH KEEPING.
IT SHINES LIKE A TREASURE
IN MY MIND.
7/23/200

HANGING ON TO THE TATTERED EDGES-
OUR CONFRONTATIONS
WHILE WE'VE BEEN APART
HAVE BEEN STORM CLOUDS
RAINING...
ON ALL MY SUNNY DAYS.
KEEPING OUT THE LIGHT
AND LEAVING MY HEART
ICY IN THE DARKNESS.
I CAN'T GET PAST
THE FEELING
THAT YOU DON'T LOVE ME
ANYMORE
AND I DON'T KNOW WHY
WE DIDN'T TRY HARDER
TO KEEP IT TOGETHER
INSTEAD OF LETTING IT
FALL APART.
IT SEEMS SO MUCH EASIER
TO LOVE
THAN LET LOVE DIE
FROM THE LACK
OF SINCERITY.
6/14/2008

I CLOSE MY EYES
AND DREAM
OF FINGERS PAINTING
ACROSS MY SKIN
A SIGH ESCAPES
INTO YOUR WARM MOUTH
AND I REMAIN MOVED
BY THE DESIRE.
2/07/2017

INSIDE MY BRAIN
YOU ARE FOUND
WRITTEN IN LOVING HAND
AMONG OUR WHISPERED PHRASES
AND I LIE CARESSING YOUR EDGES
AWAKE TO THE TEMPTATION
HIDDEN IN YOUR PAGES
2/14/2017

YOUR HEART HAS GROWN COLD
WHY WON'T YOU GIVE ME
WHAT I WANT?

I'M STANDING HERE FREEZING
COVERED IN YOUR FROST

YOU USED TO BE SO WARM
ALL I COULD FEEL WAS YOUR FIRE
NOW I SIT HERE ALL ALONE
SHIVERING IN DENIAL

BABY JUST GIVE ME
A LITTLE OF YOUR FLAME
BEFORE I BLOW OUT
1/17/2017

*INSPIRED BY LONELY SUNDAY BY REIGNWOLF

I CAME A LONG WAY FOR A SMILE
HANGING ON TO THIS FEELING
ALL THE WHILE
A CLAMOURING HEART
LIKE AN OVER USED TURNSTILE
COUNTING DOWN UNTIL I SEE YOUR FACE
12/21/2017

I WOULD CLIMB
INSIDE THIS DARKNESS
TO TOUCH YOUR FACE AGAIN
AND FEEL THE CONTOURS
UNDER MY FINGERTIPS
AS I KISS THE SOLACE
FROM YOUR LIPS
WHILE BREATHING IN
YOUR SIGHS.
12/07/2011

I'M BEARING ALL THIS PRESSURE
BECOMING SWEETER ON THE VINE
WISHING FOR FEVERISH TOUCH
TO TURN MY DESIRE IN WINE
WHILE WE'RE
PASSING ALL THESE MOMENTS
WICKED PARALLELS
FALLING DOWN OUR RABBIT HOLES
TO HIDE THE FEARS
WE KNOW SO WELL
SO WHEN, WILL WE TAKE ANOTHER'S HAND?
& LIVE BEYOND ANXIETIES MASTER PLAN
CAN WE LEARN TO LOVE AGAIN...
11/29/2017

I GET SO MAD
AT MYSELF
WHEN I MISS YOU
THINKING OF ALL
THE LOST TIMES
THAT I
SHOULD HAVE BEEN
KISSING
THE MOUTH
THAT FIRST
ENCHANTED
ME
INSTEAD
I'M LOCKED
INSIDE
OF THE MEMORY.
11/19/2017

I TRIED TO TOUCH YOUR SOUL
BUT YOU LEFT MY FINGERS STINGING
AS THE SPARK TURNED INTO FLAME
& CAUSED THIS CONSTANT CRAVING
I'M TRYING TO PULL BACK FROM IT'S HEAT
TO SAVE MY HEART FROM MELTING
ALL I FIND IS I CAN'T DENY
THE SEARING 3RD DEGREE
JUST TO SEE YOUR SMILE
IS WORTH ANY AMOUNT OF PAIN.
2/02/2014

I've cried out for solace
Has it been wasted?
fell on deaf ears
when my heart you tasted
now I need the dark to feel at ease
You've have me crawling on my knees
I am breaking under this weight
I don't become the one you hate
Without your touch I withered here
There was never anyone else
But you my dear.
3/02/2016

MY MIND IS A TRAITOR
FLOODING MY MEMORY
WITH NOSTALGIA
WHILE I CAN'T STEP AWAY
AND I DON'T WANT TO
BECAUSE I CAN FEEL YOUR SOUL
ACHING LIKE MY OWN
LOOKING FOR A HOME
A PLACE HOLDS YOUR HEART
WITH A DEEPER FEELING
BEEN WAITING FOR THE DAY
THAT HAS DRAWN THE CLOUDS AWAY
LIGHTING UP MY WORLD
IN YOUR INFINITY
I HAD CLOSED MYSELF OFF
TO STEEL THE PAIN
SO FAR AWAY
FROM THIS FEELING.
3/03/2014

I've memorized your face
A thousand times
Seen those dreams
We never seem to say
And I'm holding out
For the day
When can share
Those secret memories
It's been a long time
Standing on the outside
Of your arms
& it's lonely here
But I know I'll stay warm
Covered in these scars.
3/02/2016

FILLING UP THE HOLLOW
YOUR WORDS TORE OUT
I AM BARELY BREATHING
AND BLEEDING OUT
YOU WERE MY SOLACE
I HOPE WE'D TRY
TO BUILD A LIFE TOGETHER
BUT YOU LET LOVE DIE
STAND HERE ALONE
AS I CRY
THOUGHT YOU WERE SINCERE
BUT YOU ONLY LIED
YOU WERE THE PEACE
INSIDE THE PAIN
YOU BROKE ME OUT
TO SEE LIGHT AGAIN.
2/08/2014

THE SIGHT OF YOU
LEAVES ME QUIVERING
BUTTERFLIES EXPLODE
INSIDE MY CHEST
DANCING THEIR WAY
INTO MY WORDS
LEAVING ME UTTERING
THE MOST VULNERABLE PHRASES
HOPING YOU SEE HOW ENCHANTED
I AM BY THE MAN I SEE BEFORE ME.
2/09/2014

These walls are crumbling
I fear, I can't hold back the tide
rushing all around me
and simply won't subside

I used to count on your love for me
to hold back the crushing wave -
but now I have to question,
if it was only your skin
you were out to save.

I'm choking on the bitterness
of your uncompleted promises
drowning on the taste of our past -
sleepwalking through my world
without you in it
praying everyday you're gone
will be my last.

You took everything
I emotionally possess...
leaving me bereft.
4/27/2011

Open road
Don't know which way to go,
I used to have a destination
until my compass heart
lost the location
in this hard fought war
against the isolation
walling off my soul
& I'm so sick of trying

to find the keys to my own sanity
lost among the remnants of better days,

it makes me want to slip away
into the dark.

8/24/12

THIS LUSH GROUND
BECKONS ME DOWN
TO LIE AMONG IT'S LEAVES,
SMOTHER ME
IN THIER DARK PUNGENT BEAUTY
WHILE THE MOON LIGHTS MY WAY
& YOUR DESIRE
FILLS MY MIND.
9/18/2014

I WANT YOUR TOUCH.
I CLOSE MY EYES
AND CAN ALMOST FEEL YOUR FINGERS.
I CRAVE YOUR MOUTH,
TO TASTE THEIR WORDS
BETWEEN MY LIPS.
MY AROUSAL HEIGHTENS
WHEN EVER YOU ARE NEAR,
MY NIPPLES RAISE
AT THE SOUND OF YOUR VOICE
AND I ACHE TO TRACE
MY FANTASIES
ON YOUR SKIN
WITH MY CARESS.
YOU LEAVE MY BODY
TINGLING
WAITING
FOR YOUR LENGTH
& ENDLESS DESIRE.
2/15/2014

THIS CRAVING IS BUILDING
I CAN'T HELP BUT CLOSE MY EYES
AND MENTALLY TRACE
YOUR FRAME ONCE AGAIN
AND IT MAKES ME
WANT TO HEAR YOUR SIGH
CURVE UP THE BACK OF MY SPINE
I CATCH MY BREATH
AT THE VERY THOUGHT OF YOU.
9/15/2014

SOME PEOPLE
MAKE MY LIFE BETTER
BY JUST BEING IN IT.
HOLD QUALITIES
THAT FEEL LIKE SERENITY.
I WISH THOSE PEOPLE
COULD SEE
THEMSELVES
THROUGH MY EYES.
2016

YOU ARE THE SEA
I SWIM IN...
THE EBB & FLOW
OF THIS TEMPTATION
IS EXCRUCIATING.
MY SKIN TINGLES
AT YOUR SLIGHTEST TOUCH.
7/10/2014

TURN MY REGRETS
INTO A FUNERAL PYRE
FOR THE DAYS LONG PAST
AWAKEN MY EVERY DESIRE
FROM THE MOMENT
I TOUCH YOUR LIPS...
I WANT TO SET FIRE
TO THIS CHEMISTRY
FAN THE FLAMES
AS THEY CONSUME ME
SCREAM YOUR NAME
IN EXTASCY
INSTEAD OF CHOKING
ON THE BURNING ASHES
OF THINGS LEFT UNSAID.
6/16/14

I LOOK AT YOU
AND I CATCH MY BREATH
AS I FEEL
TEMPTATION DANCING
CLOSE TO ME
I WANT TO CLOSE MY EYES
WHILE MY THOUGHTS CAREEN
OFF MY DESIRE
TO TASTE YOUR FLESH
AND WAKE UP TO YOUR SMILE.
6/14/2014

YOU ARE THE CHINK
IN MY ARMOR
THE CRACK
IN MY BATTERED WALL
MY ONE HEART'S FRAILTY
I HELD ABOVE IT ALL
YOU'RE MY SOUND
OF THUNDER
THE LIGHTING
IN MY STORM
THE SOLACE
THAT SOOTHES MY SOUL
WHEN I'M TOO FAR
FROM HOME.
5/21/2014

I NEED YOUR FLESH
PRESSED UP AGAINST
MY SIGHS
OPEN ME UP
TO REVEAL MY DESIRE
TOUCH MY HEART
FROM THE INSIDE
STEAL MY SOUL
WITH YOUR BREATH
AND LEAVE YOUR SWEETNESS
ON MY LIPS.
5/20/2014

I ALWAYS THOUGHT YOU WERE
MY PARAMOUR
BUT NOW I FIND
THAT YOUR JUST A DOOR
TO EVERYTHING I LEFT FAR BEHIND
THERE'S NO SINCERITY TO REPLACE
THE WAY I FELL FROM GRACE
CHASING AFTER THE FANTASY
YOU LET ME BUILD UP IN MY MIND
I GAVE UP ALL I HAD
FOR JUST ONE TASTE OF YOU
AND I CAN'T SEEM TO ERASE
THAT MEMORY FROM MY VEIW.
5/07/2014

YOU'VE BEEN WALKING MY MIND
FOR AN ETERNITY
HAUNTING
MY DARK HALLS
PRESENT
IN MY SUNRISE
WHERE MY HOPE
STILL GROWS
THERE IN THE GOLDEN SILENCE
I CAN STILL HEAR
YOUR FOOTFALLS
THAT ECHO IS STILL
SO BITTERSWEET.
4/27/2014

GHOST LIKE FINGERS
CRAWL UP MY SPINE
WHISPERING YOUR NAME
INTO MY HAIR
I CRAVE YOUR FINGERS
IN THEIR PLACE
I WANT THEM
EVERYWHERE.
2/16/14

LOOKING AT THE SPACE
WHERE WE USED
TO RESIDE
TEMPTING PERFECTION
TO TEASING REJECTION
IN THE WINK
OF YOUR BLUE EYES...
BUT OH GOD
I CAN'T HELP
BUT MISS YOUR SMILE
FEELS LIKE IT'S BEEN
MUCH LONGER
THAN I WANT TO KNOW
THIS SHEET'S BARREN DISTANCE
MEASURES
EVERY TEAR STAINED MILE
I HAVE LEFT TO GO...
3/29/2014

IMAGES ON MY SCREEN
ARE WHERE MY EYES
KEEP RETURNING
WITH A LONGING
IN MY HEART
THAT LEAVES MY BODY
SHAKING
AND I KEEP WONDERING
IF THERE IS NO ERASING
ALL THE DAMAGE
THAT WE'VE DONE
AND STILL
WE KEEP ON REACHING
HOPING
THAT WE FIND
THAT THERE IS
ANOTHER WAY.
3/20/2014

Overlooking this desolation
Burned out dreams
Left too discarded
to try to save
I opened up my heart to you
And was left with
This crater full of lies
Like a broken mirror
Too tarnished
To ever really shine
These shattered memories
Bring me nothing
But pain Every time
I see your smile
A haunting reflection
Of a life I left behind...

3/15/2014

Here In the dark
I want to breathe you in
Full to the depth
Of my own volition

Indigo skies
painting my view
Held in this moment
Of loving you.
3/13/2014

STRIPPING OFF
THIS ISOLATION
BURY DEEP YOUR MEMORY
FOUND MY WAY
INSIDE THIS BOTTLE
SO I CAN FINALLY GAIN
SOME PEACE
HAUNTING VOICES ECHOING
FROM THE DARKNESS
OF MY MIND
TUMBLING DOWN
THIS HOLLOW
I KEEP WONDERING
WHY I'M ALIVE
AND STILL YOU CONTINUE
TO TAKE
EVERYTHING FROM ME
FROM BEYOND THE GRAVE
THAT WAS OUR LIFE.
3/11/2014

I do not belong here
without seeing your face
when your eyes
hold my only solace

This constant ache
My only companion
The scars a tourniquet
Around my heart.
3/11/2014

I NEVER SAID I LOVE YOU LIGHTLY...
IT WAS ALWAYS DRAGGING
A HEART SHAPED WEIGHT
BEHIND.
2014

AWAKE YET DREAMING
ALIVE BUT SCREAMING
EVERY PERSON GLIMPSED
STILL HOLDS YOUR FACE
MY BODY SHAKES
WITHDRAWING FROM YOU
LIKE AN ADDICTS CRAVING
AS MY MIND TRIES
TO DENY THE DAMAGE
I'M HANGING BY A THREAD
IN THIS NETWORK OF SCARS
PIECING BACK TOGETHER
A SHATTERED HEART.
3/09/2014

I CAN'T LIVE HERE
IN YOUR SHADOW
PALE AND ALL ALONE
THE PIECES OF YOUR STUNNING REJECTION
ARE JUST TOO SHARP TO HANG ON
BROKEN AWAY
FROM I USED TO KNOW
I'M STANDING HERE
IN THE EYE OF THE STORM
CRYING OUT
AS THIS ACID HITS MY VEINS
I'VE SPENT TOO LONG
IN YOUR GRAVITY
TO EVER BE THE SAME.
2/27/2014

POUR ME OUT
AN EMPTY VESSEL
THROWN ASIDE
MY EXTERIOR STAINED
BY THE BETRAYAL
A HOLLOW MOAN ECHOES
AT MY CORE
THE GHOST OF
FORGOTTEN JOY
LEFT SOUR IN MY MOUTH.
2/25/2014

YOU SAY I LOVE YOU
LIKE A CONSOLATION PRIZE
THERE'S NO NEED TO SUGAR COAT IT
WHEN THE GAPING WOUND STILL RESIDE
I COULD BUILD ANOTHER PEDESTAL
BUT THAT WOULD ONLY AIDE
TO MY OWN DEMISE
INSTEAD I'LL SLOWLY BACK AWAY
TRYING NOT TO CRY
AS I SLIP PAST
FATES LAST LIE.
2/23/2014

YOU ARE MY ONLY DESIRE.
MY BODY CRAVES
THE TASTE OF YOU.
THE DEEP CONVERSATION
OF SKIN ON SKIN.
MY SOUL IS ON FIRE
EVERY TIME
I SEE YOUR FACE,
YOUR MOUTH IS ALL I SEEK
TO SLOW THE BURN.
2/23/2014

THERE ARE DAYS
WHEN I WAKE
TO SEE THE SPACE
I INHABIT
AND WISH
YOU WERE NEVER IN IT
SO I WOULDN'T KNOW
THE WAY YOU KISS
ENOUGH TO MISS IT
OR HANG ON THE VERY VOCAL TONE
ONLY YOU SEEM TO ENJOY
LIKE I'M DROWNING
I WISH I NEVER KNEW
YOUR HEART
BECAUSE NOW EVERYONE
IS PAINTED
IN A LESSER SHADE.
10/31/2017

THIS LIGHT REFRACTED
NOW A MYRIAD OF DESTINYS
FALLING BEFORE OUR EYES
IN ABSTRACT GALAXIES
ONE COULD HOPE TO QUESTION
THE COMPLEXITIES
IN THE SWIRLING DUST
THAT USED TO BE OUR LIVES
10/24/2017

I FEEL LIKE I'M BROKEN APART
I CAN STILL FEEL YOUR HAND
GRASPING MY HEART
THE LONELINESS GROWS
AS THE YEARS GO BY SLOW
YOU WERE THE ONLY ONE
FROM THE VERY START.
10/23/17

I CAN FEEL RESISTANCE
WHILE YOU'RE SHINING
IN THE DISTANCE,
SO CLOSE & YET
SO FAR AWAY...
MY HEART FEELS
PULLED IN TWO,
AM I JUST
A LOVESICK FOOL?
RUNNING AFTER
FRIENDSHIP
DISGUISED AS SPARK?
10/06/2017

ADRIFT IN YOUR AFFECTION
LIKE A BOAT WITH OUT DIRECTION
YOU'RE THE VOICE I HEAR IN MY HEAD
THE APPARITION I FOLLOW FROM BED
THE INSPIRATION TO STRIVE
TO CLIMB EVEN HIGHER
ON THE DAYS I WISH I WERE DEAD
9/26/2017

CHANGE IS ON THE WIND
I THINK IT'S TIME TO BEGIN
I'M JUST NOT SURE
WHICH WAY IT'S GONNA BLOW
SO I'M COMING HOME
I SEE THE SKY DARKEN
THROUGH MY SCREEN
AND I'M NOT SURE
WHAT IT MEANS
BUT CHASING MY DREAMS
DOWN THIS OLD BROKEN ROAD
10/05/2017

THERE'S A KINK IN MY SYSTEM,
A STALL IN MY ENGINE.
I NEED TO SHAKE OFF THIS GRAVEYARD DUST,
WIPE AWAY THE COBWEBS,
& SHOO AWAY THIS DAMN GREY SKY.
A LIFE OF MORAL CELIBACY CAN BE SO BORING,
I NEED TO REMEMBER WHERE
I HID MY WICKED SMILE...
MY CREATIVITY CRAVES SOME INSPIRATION
LIKE A ROCKET SHIP
HEADING TO A FAR FLUNG NEBULA,
I JUST NEED A KICK IN THE THRUSTER.
10/01/2013

THE LIGHT SHINES
FROM WITHIN YOU
& I AM CAPTIVATED
BY THE GLOW
WRAPPING YOU
IN A WARMTH
THAT PROTECTS YOU
FROM THE COLD
LIFE'S HARSH REALITIES
JUST SEEM TO FALL AWAY
AS YOU WALK
THROUGH THIS WORLD
BRINGING JOY
FROM DAY TO DAY
I SIT HERE QUIETLY
WAITING FOR YOU
TO LOOK MY WAY
WHILE AFFECTION
TANGLES ON MY TONGUE
AND SILENTLY FADES.
9/23/12

I'VE GOT AN ITCH
THAT I CAN'T REACH
& TANGLED KNOTS
THAT HOLD MY SOUL
IN A STRANGLEHOLD
ACHING FOR RELIEF,
CAN YOU GIVE ME
WHAT I NEED
OR WITH YOUR TOUCH
WILL I COMPLETELY
COME UNDONE
WITH THE ENDORPHINS
RUNNING THROUGH ME
PAINTING MY SKIN
IN SHADES
OF BLUSHING CRIMSON.
9/15/2011

STANDING HERE
IN DESOLATION,
MY SKIN'S A DESERT
WHERE CRAVING YOUR TOUCH
BECOMES A PHYSICAL PAIN,
I'M SLIPPING DEEPER
INTO THIS DARKNESS
WHISPERING YOUR NAME,
CAN YOU HEAR ME,
I NEED TO FEEL YOU,
I'M LOOKING FOR RELIEF
WHILE MY BODY
IS PRAYING FOR RAIN.
9/13/12

SHADES OF DESIRE
COLOR MY MEMORIES
FINGERS SLICK
REMEMBERING THE FEEL
OF YOUR SKIN
THE GHOST OF A SMILE
WHISPERS IT'S PASSING
YOUR KISS REMAINS
THE SWEETEST BEGINNING.
9/11/2017

I COULD CRY,
BUT THAT WON'T HELP THIS FEELING
TRY AS I MIGHT
MY HEART JUST WON'T START HEALING
I CAN'T EXPLAIN
WHY THIS PAIN FEELS NEVER ENDING
YOU LEFT A PART OF ME DEAD INSIDE
AND I CAN'T STOP THIS GREIVING...
I'LL LOCK IT AWAY,
BURIED DEEP BELOW THE SURFACE,
ERR ON THE SIDE OF CAUTION,
SO I'LL GET HURT LESS,
FORGET YOUR NAME
LIKE SOMETHING I COULD ERRASE,
TELL MYSELF I MATTERED TO YOU
SO I WON'T FEEL LIKE MY LOVE
WAS WASTED.
1/14/2012

YOU STUNNED ME
& HELD IN A ROMANTIC HAZE
I PLACED YOU HIGH ON A PEDESTAL,
SAFE BEYOND REPROACH
I NUTURED THAT UNTARNISHED MEMORY
WHILE I SWAM IN THE DEEP

YOUR LOVE WAS MY GREATEST TREASURE
WHAT SHINED GOLDEN
TURNED FALSE ON THE SURFACE
WEIGHTED IRON CHAINS
CONSTRICTING MY HEART.
YOU GAVE ME THE BENDS
DECADES IN THE MAKING
IT ALL FELL APART,

HEARTFELT WORDS BECOMMING MY ENEMY
CAPSIZING ALL MY BELIEFS

WE WERE YOUNG
ENJOYING THE ROAR OF THE WATER,
NOW I'M SWALLOWING YOUR WAKES
WITH MY TEARS & DROWNING

I WAS ENCHANTED BY THE MAN
I ALWAYS KNEW YOU COULD BE
NEVER KNOWING THAT SHIMMERING GHOST,
THE PARAMOUR THAT I LOVE
WOULD BE WHAT DESTROYS ME.
9/05/2011

I PRAY
YOU STAY
PRESENT THIS MOMENT
WHILE THE WORLD
RATTLES AND CRIES
VIVING TO STEAL
EVERY SECOND OF TIME
AS I ABIDE
STANDING ASIDE
WAITING TO FIND
MY SANCTUARY
SHINING
BEHIND YOUR EYES
9/05/2013

I SEE YOU SMILE
AND I LINGER
HERE
SINKING DEEP
INTO THIS EMOTION
LICKING THE TASTE
OF JOY
FROM MY LIPS
AND SAVORING
THE FLAVOR
8/07/2017

IN THE BLUE LIGHT
SHE COMES TO YOUR COAXING,
AWAKENS IN THE MOONLIGHT
TO YOUR SEDUCTIVE GAZE,
THE GHOST OF YOUR SMILE
IS MIRRORED ON HER FACE,
SHE IS PURRING
THIS WILD ONE
REACHING OUT
TO GRASP YOUR SIN
WITH BOTH HANDS
AND BRING YOU
TO YOUR KNEES,
BY THE TIME YOU SEE THAT LOOK
IN HER EYES
YOUR HEART
HAS ALREADY BEEN CAPTURED.
9/04/12

I OFTEN WONDER
HOW IT FEELS
KNOWING YOU CARRY MY HEART
IN YOUR BACK POCKET
& HOPE WHEN YOU FEEL DEFEATED
THAT YOU ARE COMFORTED
BY THE THOUGHT
THAT WE ARE ALWAYS AS CLOSE
AS A HEARTBEAT IN TIME.
9/03/2011

I CAN'T SLEEP IN THIS STIFLING HEAT
WHEN I WANT YOUR HANDS ALL OVER ME,
I'VE GOT A CRAVING
AND NEED TO FEED MY DISEASE,
WITHOUT THE TASTE OF YOUR MOUTH
I CAN'T SEEM TO BREATHE...
DESPERATELY SEEKING
A SOOTHING REPRIEVE
WHEN THE FEEL OF YOUR SKIN
BRINGS MY ONLY RELIEF
I'M UNDER YOUR SPELL
AND I CAN'T BREAK FREE,
DESIRE BURNS THROUGH MY VEINS
& YOUR WICKED FORM
IS FANNING THE FLAMES.
9/04/12

YOU'RE MY ADRENALINE,
THE RUSH THAT PUSHES ME
TO GREATER THINGS...
YOU ARE THE INTOXICATION
THAT AWAKES ALL MY SENSES...
WITHOUT YOU
THE WORLD IS DEEPER SHADES OF GREY
AND BITTER TO THE TASTE.
YOU ARE MY SOULS ONLY CRAVING.
9/03/2013

FLIPPING THE PAGES
OF OUR TARNISHED PAST,
LOOKING FOR THE CLUES
TO WHAT WE LACKED,
RUBBING MY FINGERS
OVER OUR HISTORY,
WIPING AWAY
THE TEAR STAINED DAYS
TO SEE WHAT REMAINS...
ALL THESE MEMORIES,
HELD IN MYSTERY,
HEARTFELT MOMENTS
KEPT SO MUM,
PULLED APART
IN INDECISION,
HOW CAN I EVER FEEL
ANYTHING
BUT LOVINGLY NUMB.
8/30/12

I AM FRAGILE
HELD SO FAR
FROM YOUR HEART,
MY SHELL IS CRACKED
OVER YEARS OF WEAR
SO YOU CAN SEE
DISCOLORATION
FROM TRYING TO HOLD
YOUR SECRETS SO TIGHTLY.
I NEED YOUR ARMS TO HEAL,
YOUR LIPS TO WHISPER
MY NAME
AS A SALVE
TO KEEP ME
FROM BREAKING
& REPAIR
THE WOMAN
YOU AWAKENED.
8/28/2011

I'M DRAGGING UNDER
THIS SAD RELIQUARY
OF ALL WE ARE
AND ALL WE HOPED TO BE
BROKE MY RIBS
TO FIT INSIDE
SUCH A SIMPLE HOME
WHERE MY HEART
ONCE RESIDED
TO THE HOPE
WE BURNED IN EFFIGY.
8/13/2017

HOLD ME TIGHTLY
PULL MY SHOULDER BACK
MY NECK EXPOSED
YOUR HUNGRY MOUTH
LEAVING MY BREATHING RAGGED
THIS IS HOW I SEE US
AS I CLOSE MY EYES.
7/31/2017

PETRICHOR~
MY SOUL IS THIRSTY
YOU'RE MY PETRICHOR
LIGHTENING
MY OZONE
ELECTRIC
SPARKS FLY
WHENEVER WE'RE TOGETHER
I TREMBLE WITH EXHILARATION
HELD FAST BY DESIRE
I AM YOUR LIGHTENING ROD
MY BODY SINGS
WITH THE CURRENT
APART
COLD METAL
QUIET STEEL
AWAITING CONTACT.
~1/25/2008~

OCTOPUS~
A KOI IN A CRYSTAL BOWL
I SWIM IN MEMORIES
YOU'VE CLUNG TO MY HEART
LIKE AN OCTOPUS
I FEEL THE SQUEEZE
EVERY TIME
I SEE YOUR PHOTOGRAPH.
~1/25/2008~

YOU ARE THE CRAVING
I CAN'T DEVOUR
WHEN I LOOK AT YOU
I CAN'T SWALLOW
WHEN ALL I WANT
IS YOUR FLAVOR
ON MY TONGUE
I WANT TO GET PAST
THIS RESPECTFUL HESITATION
AND LEAVE THIS TEMPTATION
IN THE PLACE WHERE OUR CLOTHES
BECOME UNDONE.
7/16/2017

NOSTALGIA CLINGS
TOO STRONG & HEADY
DUSTING MY MEMORY
WITH IT'S ILLUSIONS
DULLING MY SENSES
& LEAVING ME DRUNK
ON YOUR GAZE...
2016

BEEN STANDING HERE
WITH MILES TO GO
IN THE FALLING RAIN
WISHING FOR A PRAYER
WHILE MY HEART'S
STILL ON A PLANE
FOLLOWING THOSE
FOOTSTEPS BACK
TWENTY ODD YEARS
OF PAIN
BUT DAMN
WHAT I'D GIVE
TO BE BACK
ON RUBY LANE
3/27/2016

ABOUT THE AUTHOR

    Jenifer Stroud is a Pacific Northwest Poet & Music Enthusiast. She can be found cleverly hidden in the retail sector by day and at music venues enjoying her true passion in her free time.
    Her poetry comes from the places all good music comes from, the depths of her heart and the darkest corners of the soul. Within these pages her truth is left on display in all its glimmering and tarnished beauty.
    Buy the ticket & take the ride. Enjoy every seductive curve & learn to let go of the wheel.
    Her words will fall as easily as the rains in Cascadia & will surprise you.

Made in the USA
Columbia, SC
14 October 2024